American Indians

THE
ALGONQUIN

by N.C. Barnes

WELCOME TO
DiscoverRoo!

This book is filled with videos, puzzles, games, and more! Scan the QR codes* while you read, or visit the website below to make this book pop.

popbooksonline.com/Algonquin

abdobooks.com

Published by Pop!, a division of ABDO, PO Box 398166, Minneapolis, Minnesota 55439. Copyright © 2025 by Abdo Consulting Group, Inc. International copyrights reserved in all countries. No part of this book may be reproduced in any form without written permission from the publisher. DiscoverRoo™ is a trademark and logo of Pop!.

Printed in the United States of America, North Mankato, Minnesota.

052024
082024

Cover Photo: The Canadian Press/Associated Press, Shutterstock Images
Interior Photos: Shutterstock Images, Getty Images, Alamy Stock Photo, Wikimedia, Wikimedia/ Encyclopedia Virginia
Editor: Emily Dreher
Series Designer: Colleen McLaren

Library of Congress Control Number: 2023947497

Publisher's Cataloging-in-Publication Data

Names: Barnes, N.C., author.

Title: The Algonquin / by N.C. Barnes

Description: Minneapolis, Minnesota : Pop!, 2025 | Series: American Indians | Includes online resources and index

Identifiers: ISBN 9781098246181 (lib. bdg.) | ISBN 9781098246747 (ebook)

Subjects: LCSH: Algonquin Indians--Juvenile literature. | American Indians--Juvenile literature. | Indians of North America--Juvenile literature. | Indigenous peoples--Social life and customs--Juvenile literature. | Cultural anthropology--Juvenile literature.

Classification: DDC 973.0497--dc23

*Scanning QR codes requires a web-enabled smart device with a QR code reader app and a camera.

TABLE OF CONTENTS

CHAPTER 1

WHO ARE THE ALGONQUIN?

Before European **settlers** came to North America, the land was wild and open. It was populated by American Indians. Each group had its own languages and culture. Culture is the customs, arts, and ideas of a group of people.

WATCH A VIDEO HERE!

The Algonquin people believe it is important to work together.

The Algonquin are part of the Anishinaabe peoples. This group also includes the Ojibwe, Delaware, Mississauga, Odawa, and Potawatomi tribes.

ALGONQUIN HOMELANDS

CANADA

ONTARIO

QUEBEC

Lake Superior

Ottawa River

St. Lawrence River

Lake Huron

Lake Michigan

Lake Ontario

Lake Erie

UNITED STATES

HISTORICAL ALGONQUIN TERRITORY

The Algonquin lived in specific parts of the highlighted area.

ATLANTIC OCEAN

The Algonquin people have lived in North America for thousands of years. **Elders** of the tribe say they have been there since the beginning of time. Historically, Algonquins lived near the St. Lawrence River and the Ottawa River. These rivers flow through Ontario and Quebec in Canada. It is heavily forested, rocky land with shallow soil.

Many Algonquin people lived near the Great Lakes.

Some Algonquin people refer to themselves as Omàmìwininì. It means "down river people."

Long ago, Algonquins lived in bands of 100 to 300 people. The bands were led by women and came together in the summer. In the winter, bands divided into smaller groups of one- or two-family **clans**. They stayed in a camp together for the season.

All Algonquins are members of a clan. Clans are named after an animal, such as a loon. This animal watches over and protects clan members.

Loons are famous for their haunting calls.

CHAPTER 2

HISTORICAL LIFE

Algonquin people lived in wigwams. These were dome-shaped homes made from birch bark, animal skins, and tree branches. There was a hole in the top of a wigwam to let out smoke from a fire. In the winter, Algonquins covered the floor with tree branches and animal skins.

LEARN MORE HERE!

Most birch bark wigwams were about ten feet (3m) wide and eight to ten feet (2.4 to 3m) tall.

DID YOU KNOW?

When moving from place to place, Algonquins took the birch bark and animal skins with them. They left the branch frames.

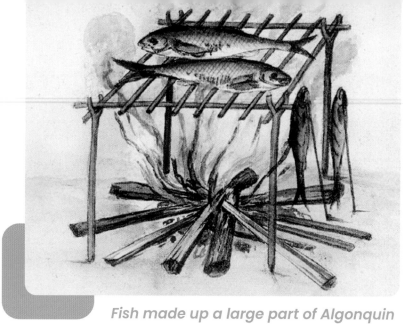

Fish made up a large part of Algonquin people's diet.

The Algonquins did some farming. However, most locations had summers that were too short to grow much food. Instead, Algonquins would hunt, fish, and gather their food. They gathered wild rice, berries, and maple tree sap. They hunted moose, caribou, bears, deer, porcupines, and beavers.

Algonquins lived around fresh water. Fishing gave them lots of food. They were expert fishers. Algonquins used large traps called fish fences in rivers.

They even fished at night in canoes with a bright torch at the front. A person at the front of the canoe speared fish that were attracted to the light. In the winter, Algonquins ice fished from holes in lakes.

Hunting and fishing required Algonquins to work as a team.

Algonquin people deeply respect all parts of nature.

Algonquin people made clothes from animal skins. They used deerskin for **tunics**. Women wore longer tunics than men. In the summer, tunics were sleeveless.

When it got cold, people wore more layers, such as leggings, long robes, mittens, hoods, and fur caps. They wore tall moccasins in winter and low moccasins during warmer weather.

Moccasin designs were unique to each community.

CHAPTER 3

BELIEFS AND TRADITIONS

Algonquins do not believe in land ownership. They believe that the Creator and Mother Earth trusted them with the land they live on. It is their responsibility to care for the land. They never hunt or farm the land too much.

EXPLORE
LINKS
HERE!

Algonquin people gathered wild sage for traditional practices.

Algonquin people started using guns to hunt after the Europeans came to North America.

MAKING A CANOE

Birch bark is strong, flexible, and waterproof. It's the perfect material to build a boat. First, the bark is peeled from the tree and dried. Then it is stretched over a cedar-wood frame. The canoe is sealed with spruce **resin**. Master builders passed down canoe-building skills.

Algonquin clothes, food, and homes were all made from products of the earth. Birch bark was one of the most important materials for Algonquin people. June and July were

Birchbark canoes are lightweight and strong.

the best times to peel the bark from

birch trees. They made their homes,

boxes, and dishes from this bark. One

of their most impressive creations is the

birchbark canoe.

Algonquin people shared their teachings through song, art, and stories.

The Algonquin people followed the teachings of the Seven Grandfathers. The teachings were Love, Honesty, Truth, Respect, Bravery, **Humility**, and Wisdom. These lessons guided Algonquin on how to care for their land and people.

Elders in the tribe taught children about the Seven Grandfathers. Children also learned about the Great Spirit, who was the creator of everything.

Algonquin kids helped the clan by gathering firewood, food, and water. They cleaned and helped make clothes and meals. Children also had lots of time to play and connect with nature.

Children helped gather wild rice from bodies of water.

CHAPTER 4

ALGONQUIN PEOPLE TODAY

Algonquins faced many challenges when European **settlers** arrived in North America. At first, the Algonquin shared their goods and knowledge with Europeans. In the 1600s they traded furs to the French for guns, cloth, and axes.

COMPLETE AN ACTIVITY HERE!

Some white Americans photographed American Indians to document the culture they thought was fading.

Unfortunately, diseases from the

Europeans spread to the Algonquins.

These diseases killed many.

Historical regalia made from animal skins, beads, and other natural materials was usually worn for special occasions.

Algonquins tried to build trust

and friendship with the Europeans.

They signed **treaties** in hopes of

protecting the land they loved so much.

But eventually, Europeans forced them off their homeland and onto **reservations**. By the late 1800s, Algonquins weren't allowed to speak their own language or learn their teachings.

The Europeans' arrival changed the landscape of North America forever.

Despite challenges, Algonquins

worked hard to protect their culture

and history. Today, most Algonquins

Powwows often feature traditional Algonquin songs and drum music.

still live on reservations in Ontario and

Quebec. **Elders** who protected their

culture are **revitalizing** their language

and traditions by teaching them to

children again.

Algonquins wear traditional regalia at American Indian celebrations.

Algonquin **clans** come together for powerful gatherings called powwows. Powwows are an American Indian tradition. They celebrate Algonquin culture with dancing, food, music, and **spiritual** healing. People of different

American Indian nations host powwows all over North America.

American Indians have always shared their culture through spoken stories. Algonquins will continue to care for their land, people, and history as time goes on.

In some American Indian stories, a turtle holds up all land.

MAKING CONNECTIONS

TEXT-TO-SELF

Algonquin children learned about the teachings of the Seven Grandfathers. Which teaching would you want to learn about? Please explain your answer.

TEXT-TO-TEXT

Have you read about another American Indian nation? How is their culture similar to or different from the Algonquin people?

TEXT-TO-WORLD

The Algonquin people celebrate and share their culture and history during powwows. What are other ways to celebrate culture?

GLOSSARY

clan — a group of people tracing descent from a common ancestor.

elder — a person having authority because of age or experience.

humility — the absence of any feelings of being better than others.

reservation — a piece of land set aside by the government for American Indians to live on.

resin — a sticky substance produced by evergreen trees.

revitalize — to give new life.

settler — a person who moves with a group of others to live in a new country or area. A place where settlers live is called a settlement.

spiritual — having to do with people's beliefs in things, such as the soul, nature, and what happens after death.

treaty — an official agreement.

tunic — a knee-length garment.

INDEX

DiscoverRoo!
ONLINE RESOURCES

This book is filled with videos, puzzles, games, and more! Scan the QR codes* while you read, or visit the website below to make this book pop.

popbooksonline.com/Algonquin

*Scanning QR codes requires a web-enabled smart device with a QR code reader app and a camera.